Our Journey into Unschooling:

A Look Back From the Finish Line—A Practical Guide for Prospective Unschoolers

ISBN: 978-1-967608-01-0 (paperback)
ISBN: 978-1-967608-00-3 (ebook)

Front photograph and cover image by Maya Gouliard.
Book Design by Maya Gouliard.

First Printing 2025.

www.mayagouliard.com
Mayagouliard@gmail.com

Calmillusion PRESS
INDEPENDENTLY PUBLISHED

This is dedicated to the ones I love. This memoir is as much by the kids as it is for them, we lived and learned all of this together.

To my crew for life — KTPA

Love, Mom

Table of Contents

Introduction

And those who were seen dancing were thought to be insane by those who could not hear the music.

- FRIEDRICH NIETZSCHE

Did I start my parenting journey with the expectation that I would be an unschooler? Absolutely not. In fact, a year before I had my first child, I thought I might never want to have children at all. Life has thrown me curveballs left and right, and most of the time I just swung and saw what would happen.

Each choice I made was the best I thought I could make at the time with the information I had in the moment. The thing about information is that there is always more out there. Educating myself along the way, I learned so much. I learned what others had done. I learned what I appreciated and what I disagreed with. I learned what my own opinions were.

I learned all of that **after** my years of being traditionally educated in a public-school setting.

Education is life long. And my fear is that often schools kill the curiosity we all have naturally. It defines education in such a slim way that we forget that learning happens when a baby nuzzles in eating for the first time, when toddling steps make us fall down and get back up again - all of life is learning, not just school.

Our family's decision to unschool was not made in an instant. It wasn't made while my husband and I sat dreamy eyed as newlyweds planning our lives together. It was a journey of discovery that centered on who I was, who our family was, and who I wanted our children to be.

Each and every family who unschools is going to define it a bit differently, so let's start with what mine is, and then you can continue to read about how I reached this definition.

Unschooling is child-led education through play, support, and love.

My School Experience

The whole educational and professional training system is a very elaborate filter, which just weeds out people who are too independent, and who think for themselves, and who don't know how to be submissive, and so on — because they're dysfunctional to the institutions.

- NOAM CHOMSKY

Any study about choices made as an adult should look back at the history and foundation of the person making the choices. So, let us begin in 1980. I was in first grade.

Clack, clickety, clack. I loved the sound of the marble running down the racetrack I built, and watching it hit the carpet, then guessing how far it would go before it slowed to a stop. I spent the majority of my school days building with blocks. I had a drive to build the biggest, fastest, longest ramp for racing marbles. Every day I would spend the morning stacking and building and every afternoon I would race my marbles.

The principal at our grade school was a hippie and had installed an alternative learning program called options. Parents chose between:

Option A- A classic classroom, large desk in front of room with chalkboard and teacher facing many small desks for the children. All lined up and facing forward.

Option B- A more relaxed room with some open spaces and a balance between classroom learning at desks and learning on carpets and such. This is very similar to what most classrooms look like today.

Option C- This is where the magic happens. These classrooms were built differently. First, the classes were grouped with two grades together 1-2, 3-4 and 5-6. Second, there were two teachers taking care of both classrooms, they worked together, and children moved between the rooms regularly. Third, there were very few desks. The spaces had lots of tables to encourage working together, there were lots of learning centers with books and learning tools. Math and reading were taught in smaller groups of children at similar levels rather than to the whole classroom at large.

My mother had chosen Option C. I asked her recently why she made the choice. She said because when she visited the classrooms, she liked seeing the children working together, and that those classrooms had the best teachers.

First and second grade went swimmingly for me. The main goal at that age generally is about learning to get along with others. Third grade is when the problems started appearing. It was the first time I heard "she is not living up to her potential," in a parent teacher conference. My friends were flying past me on times tables and reading classics while I was still reading Tintin comics and Choose Your Own Adventure books.

Fifth grade is when it became obvious that I was struggling. It is a whole different story if we also look at what was happening in my life outside of the classroom, and I thought to leave that for another book, but the instability of my home life played a key factor in how I raised my kids, so let's take an overview here.

My parents got divorced when I was three. From that point on, their relationship was extremely contentious; court cases abounded. My little sister and I spent every Thursday and every other weekend at Dad's house, and the rest of the time at Mom's. In the span of ten years, my mother got married, my father got married, my father got divorced again, and my father got married again. All of this happened as I kept tabs on where and when my sister and I were to be where, as our parents didn't speak to each other. A honk on the horn meant it was time to get in Dad's car. So, let's simplify it and say, there was a lot going on at home.

However, if we just look at the days in school, there were enough issues. I couldn't sit quietly, and although the classroom allowed us to move around, there were many times we were expected to be quiet — I couldn't. There were assignments due — I didn't get them finished.

The teachers had a system that if you had to be asked to follow the expectations your name would go on the board. If you had to be asked again, a check mark would be added. If you had three check marks, you stayed after school for 15 minutes. Let's just say, I never had to deal with the after-school rush of kids visiting and walking home. I was always sitting in the quiet room working on the assignments I had to finish.

It was actually much simpler for me to finish them in the room by myself without the distractions and the time limit. As an adult I look back and know that I have ADHD. I am a textbook case. But we didn't have mental health professionals in schools in the 80's. And so, I made my way through grade school, being social and getting most of the assignments done after school while sitting in an empty classroom.

"She has so much potential, if only she would put the work in." It was literally on every report card from 3rd grade on.

Junior High was a new canvas. A new chance for me. In the first semester I worked hard, paid attention in class, worked on assignments in class and generally did well. When I brought the report card home, I was proud of my all A's and a B. Mom was not, she said, "what can we do to bring the B up?"

I remember the pain in my chest as I realized all of my hard work and I still felt she was disappointed in me. My stepsister was going to a fancy school for smart people (I had not wanted to go, we shared a room, and she cried every night about how hard it was, so when I took the test, I got 41%.)

My stepfather was a history professor. My dad was a lawyer, and my mom had been a teacher for a few years before she became a stay-at-home mother. I was expected to do well in school and go to a good college. I was expected to get all A's. To want to get all A's. I didn't.

My broken little rebellious heart told me, "Who cares what they want? Not me." And my next report card was all B's with one A.

It slowly degraded, until by sophomore year in High School I was a general C student. I was very actively involved in the classroom, and that is what saved me. I was very good at getting enough answers to skirt by on tests from what we learned in class, but I never did work outside the classroom. I rarely read the assigned reading, and I rarely finished papers or other assignments. I clocked out at the end of the school day, and didn't look back.

I remember one day in Spanish all of the kids were talking about something going on that night in the auditorium. "You'll be there, right Maya?"

I had no idea what they were talking about. Turns out, there was an honor roll event for all of the kids in the school who had good grades. When I informed them that I hadn't been on the honor roll since 7th grade they were all genuinely shocked. I appeared to be a good student, but only because I was invested during class.

Insecurities plagued me. Why couldn't I just do what was expected? Either I was broken, or the school system was broken. The answers to this battled inside me my whole childhood.

Falling Out of School

> We destroy the love of learning in children, which is so strong when they are small, by encouraging and compelling them to work for petty and contemptible rewards, gold stars, or papers marked 100 and tacked to the wall or A's on report cards, or honor rolls, or dean's lists, or Phi Beta Kappa keys, in short, for the ignoble satisfaction of feeling that they are better than someone else.
>
> -JOHN HOLT

Let's jump ahead now to my early motherhood years.

Fast forward to the age of nineteen. I was a part-time community college student, on and off again dating a pretty awful guy, due to insecurities we don't need to get into here. I found myself pregnant, and when I told the guy, he said, "Well, you're going to get an abortion right?" My answer was no. He didn't stick around.

Fast forward to twenty-two as a single mother working as a full-time day waitress. I met the love of my life in the restaurant we both worked in. Hard-working, brilliant, stoic, and the kind of person everyone wishes they got the chance to know better. He doesn't let many

15

people close, and I am still so glad that he is mine. We married when I was twenty-three.

Fast forward two years and we have a beautiful family with K— four and T— one. I drove past a 'for rent' sign on a campus restaurant and suddenly we owned a restaurant with two children. One year later, I am pregnant with P— and we give up the restaurant. But that is another story.

Fast forward another year, K— is now in kindergarten, T— is two and I just gave birth to P—. We live in a tiny house that my father calls a hovel. There is a break-even point financially with three children at home where going to work makes absolutely no financial sense. You cannot make enough to cover childcare. And so, it was at this point that I quit working. J— took on more jobs to cover the difference.

Here we will slow down, because it is our first look into the school experience for our children. K— went to kindergarten while I hung out with the little ones at home. We quickly noticed a common concern I hear from many parents who have come to me over the years - picking up bad behavior. K— came home tired, grumpy and mean. My sweet girl was suddenly angry and often took it out on her siblings.

Years later another homeschooling friend told me something that really is key here. She said that she loved homeschooling because of the deeper relationships her children were able to build. While her kids were in public schools, after they got home, they had just enough time to fight with each other, do homework, eat and go to bed. When her kids were homeschooled, they still would fight, but they had time to make up and play some, before they had to eat and go to bed.

But at the time, I had no idea of these things. When J— and I discussed our options, homeschooling didn't even show up on our list. We looked at all of the private schools in town. They had smaller class sizes, and this felt like a fix to a large key piece of the problem. But holy mackerel were they expensive. We finally found one that would let her go for half days. After all, I went to half day kindergarten, we all did back in the 70's, why can't she?

J— picked up another part time job, I learned how to use food pantries, and she went to a small Christian private school. She loved it. We loved it. But over the summer we discussed other options. Less expensive options.

I still live in the town I grew up in. I thought, if I could get her into the school I went to, she would be able to enjoy the freedom of Option C. I petitioned the school, and it was approved that although we didn't live in the swanky, professor heavy neighborhood around the school, she could attend.

Her first-grade experience there was not like mine. The school no longer had options, and although it is likely the best public grade school in the area (money does that,) K— struggled to learn to read. I wasn't worried about that, but K— was. She stressed about how she did on tests, worrying about failing and disappointing her teacher.

During these last few years, I had been working with T— doing fun learning workbooks at home, he loved them. We went to playgroups with baby P— and him. K— joined us when she wasn't in school, and we all enjoyed our family time together. J— said one day, T— loves those little workbooks, maybe you should just homeschool him. My ignorant mind pictured a woman in an ankle length jean dress and long braid. However, one of the other parents in our playgroup was a homeschooler and she was eye opening to my assumptions of what defined a homeschooler. She told us about a non-sectarian homeschool group called HOUSE, that was supportive of people who chose to homeschool for non-religious reasons.

I let that information settle in, and when halfway through K— 's first grade year, things just got too hard; she was crying at home because she couldn't read, because she wasn't smart enough. My heart broke and I thought, let's just keep her home and see what happens.

This is where I will introduce a classic homeschool term: *Falling out of school.* These are the homeschoolers who didn't homeschool for religious reasons, or because they knew all along that they wanted something different for their children. These are the parents who realize that the school system is not working for their children and are trying to figure it out as they go. There are many of us, and each journey is different. I didn't that day say, "Well, let's just unschool them." I didn't even know what it was.

Curriculums & Religion

Trusting children, and ourselves, may be one of the biggest hurdles to fully embracing unschooling. After all, most of us have been schooled—and those schooled beliefs run deep.

- KERRY MCDONALD

In 2001 the internet was not what it is today. We had a computer in our home because I had won it from a radio station. It had AOL and although we used it for emails and writing papers, finding information was not the simple 'do a quick google search' it is today.

The library was a great help in finding books on the principles behind homeschooling. I read a ton of the books on their homeschooling shelf, including a great one called Teenage Liberation Handbook which was my first introduction to the word unschooling. I took information in, but I was looking for a curriculum for teaching my first grader at home.

Luckily, I had learned that there was a family down the street who was homeschooling. That mother shared her Rainbow Resource Book, the must-have ordering list of all homeschoolers before the internet, and told me about A Beka. This was a Christian homeschooling curriculum set up by subject with small packets the child worked through. We bought the whole set for second grade and started K— on it right away.

She was done with her assignments within an hour, sometimes even half an hour each day. This gave us time to spend together, and she was reading within a few weeks. She had the knowledge but needed to remove the strain.

We also had time to join the secular homeschool group H.O.U.S.E.. It stood for Home Oriented Unique Schooling Experience. I remember clearly how nervous I felt sitting at one of my first Play days with HOUSE. Families who had been doing this for years, parents who were comfortable in their choices. Next to them I felt like a duck out of water.

The kids fit in right away, running and playing. I was the opposite of my true self; I was quiet and listened. Slowly opening up to a few people and finally making some friends.

There were two main homeschool groups in our county, HOUSE and La Casa. The other group were Christian homeschoolers. Many of the people in HOUSE were also Christians (our family included, I was still regularly attending Church back then) but they had chosen to homeschool for other reasons, and they were accepting of other cultures, for example one of my closest friends in HOUSE back then was a Muslim woman.

Any curriculum available was heavily Christian. The Christians in America had paved the way for homeschoolers and stood up for laws that protected the choice to educate how an individual wanted. I was surrounded by so many unique people who were on the fringes of society. I was introduced to many Libertarians, Extreme Christians, parents dealing with children with life threatening allergies, children with autism.

My childhood had thrown me into a lot of settings where I learned to adapt, and this was nothing new to me. I learned to find what I had in common with these people. And there was always something. Most often, it was that we all loved our children. And that can be enough to look past some major differences sometimes.

So, although the homeschool landscape was heavily Christian, I found a small group of like-minded folks, homeschooling because they were unhappy with the system, and wanted to enjoy their time with their kids.

I started reading every homeschooling book at the library, especially ones that weren't Christian based. I soaked it all in and took bits and pieces of what resonated with me. Different ideas planted new seeds, and my own educational philosophy began to bloom.

We went to HOUSE group events, and I watched other families and what they did, and let these ideas sink in too. At this time, I was busy packing up and chasing babies and toddlers, but I brought little K— to the events and although she was still super young, we began to feel like a part of the group.

One sunny warmer spring day, where the bite in the air had just gotten kind enough to only wear sweatshirts, we went to a math event at an older HOUSE family's home in one of the rich neighborhoods. The event was definitely above K— 's level, many of the parents were professors or such, and the kids were at least 4th grade and above, but we were welcomed and offered a look through two boxes of curriculum books they were giving away because they were finished with them.

I chose a few, but one changed my life. It is amazing how the smallest things can impact you. You might not even realize it until years after the fact. The book was a large, heavy text called *Spelling Power*. It was a huge tome that was basically filled with every spelling list a person could need from 'at, cat, bat,' to college level spelling. It had a bright orange heavy paper cover that was already banged up from use and the pages were held together with the black plastic binder clips that many schools use. That day, it went into the slew of toys and sippi cups on the floor of our beat-up minivan with pink duct-tape holding the broken window on.

Our Journey into Unschooling

When I unloaded the book from the car with all of our other items and placed it on our shelf of books, I had no idea that it would teach me so much more than spelling.

Spelling Power

Play is often talked about as if it were a relief from serious learning. But for children play is serious learning. Play is really the work of childhood.

- FRED ROGERS

It was spring of 2002. I had implemented something I loved; all of us sat at the table to learn together. I called it 'table time.' I can hear a collective groan still to this day in my head from my kids at the name choice.

I set everyone up at the table with the schoolwork they had for the day. K— was in third grade, T— was finishing up kindergarten, and P— was just about to turn 3. I usually set P— up with some coloring pages and then worked with T— and K— on their list of learning.

We were doing what most homeschoolers do: School at Home. Trying to mimic the learning environment we are familiar with but in a home setting. In the moment it feels so very different. We are doing it in a loving space. We are doing work specifically for the child. We are able to give support because there are less students. But it still looks like school as we have known it from our own childhood.

Once a week I gave them a spelling test. The magical afore-mentioned *Spelling Power* is making its appearance — pay attention. The book had levels and placement tests. You would read a list of words off and have them spell them, if they got enough correct move up, if they got too many wrong move down, if they got exactly the correct number wrong, you were at the appropriate level for their current skills. And so, we had tested their levels, and they were working on their spelling lists. I did what I remembered, having them write a sentence with the words, practice writing them out. They did just fine at it.

Then, one morning as the birds chirped through the windows and the warm sunshine filtered through our small window, P— had had enough. She wanted to go to the park. K— and T— also wanted to, but I enforced the table time rule. We sit here until we finish, then we can go to the park. I felt awful inside, but I was in charge.

At almost 3 years old, P— could just see over the top of the table. I never enforced her sitting there, she was just coloring, so she would often go play with toys or dance around in the living room. But not this day. She wanted to go to the park. The tension in the air was getting to me. We lived in the same tiny house, a 700 square foot house that felt a bit claustrophobic when children weren't getting along. I had to spend as much time talking P— down as I did helping K— and T—. And then, in a classic toddler outburst, P— came to the table and with her arms outstretched reached for everything and swiped it off the table. K— and T— were not happy, in the chaos of crayons, pencils, worksheets and books all over the floor, I broke.

"Enough." I declared. "We are taking some time off. After all I'm in charge and you are right, it is a beautiful day." I packed them all into the car and we spent the rest of the morning at the park. They ran, and I reset.

I needed the break too. We would take a month off. It will be our Spring Break. I used the reasoning that we would still be doing schoolwork during the summer, so we could afford the extra days off for now.

We spent the time having fun. We went to the library, we went to the parks, we met friends, we watched TV. And then, I decided it was time to get back to table time.

Enough time had passed I thought, we better just retake the spelling placement tests. We will treat it like the fresh beginning of a new year. Reading the words off, we slowly passed where they had been, we moved to the next list, and the next. Both K— and T— were at least 4 spelling levels above where they had been! And all we did last month was have fun. My mind for the first time opened up to the real deep concept of unschooling - learning through life and through enjoyment.

But societal biases, personal history, parental expectations, and personal insecurities kept me on the path of trying to find an answer for them that worked in the system we were familiar with.

Should We Stay or Should We Go?

Kids who are in school just visit life sometimes, and then they have to stop to do homework or go to sleep or get to school on time. They are constantly reminded they are preparing for real life while being isolated from it.

— SANDRA DODD

The next few years were full of constant motion and change. I had our fourth child; we moved into a larger home. The old house was gorgeous, and so much more spacious, but it had been empty for years. The pipes had been frozen and our first months there were busy cutting back weeds, turning water on and off so we could fill the pot to boil pasta or flush the toilet, and then turn it off again before the spray of water from the pipes flooded the stairway. We rented, and it was in our price range. Jon worked all of the time. We made do, and I loved the house for the location and the bones it had. Before long, the pipes were fixed and good to go. The kids lovingly named our home Bob.

K—, T—, and now P— too, were in and out of school. I was unhappy with the state of things at the schools.

While, occasional highlights were amazing, the overall experience was not.

I was still so young and unsure of myself. I had been in such a constant state of figuring it out day by day that there was little time to really consider choices. I began making lists as I thought through what was best for the kids.

When the kids were in school the lists became very long. Here is a mock example:

1. Getting everyone up and out the door is a fight
2. Testing makes K— cry at night because she is worried that she will fail causing her school to not get the money it needs.
3. T— is made to sit at his desk and do extra work because he is too fast finishing assigned sheets. They won't let him just go quietly and work on a puzzle even
4. Other students are setting bad examples
5. The class sizes are too large
6. I miss them
7. Teachers teach to the class at large

8. There are tons of busy work homework on top of a whole day away from home
9. Not enough recess time
10. Not enough time outside
11. Not enough time with the family
12. Not enough play
13. Etc, etc, etc

My list of reasons I chose to put the kids back in school was always the same:

1. I am so tired
2. I am insecure that I will be able to teach them correctly

All of our kids spent some time in public schools. K— spent the most, all the way from kindergarten to some high school. She, as all oldest, was our Guinea pig. And she led the way as we tried different schools, different homeschool curriculums, different ideologies. T— also tried different schools, private schools, different curriculums.

Slowly, I realized that my problems were with the system, and no matter how much we tried to make it work and fit what we wanted, it would never change; it didn't matter which city, school, or teacher we had.

It was during this time of uncertainty that I did my best to learn all I could, and since I am a social being, I did it with a group of parents. I chose my favorite of all of the books I have read so far and invited other parents in HOUSE to join me to go through it and discuss. The book was *A Charlotte Mason Companion: Personal Reflections on the Gentle Art of Learning.*

Charlotte Mason Book Club

Children learn from anything and everything they see. They learn wherever they are, not just in special learning places.

-JOHN HOLT

These few years were full of different attempts to do what was best for our own family in the moment. We had a few great semesters of school with fantastic teachers, K— 's fourth grade (she spent three quarters of the year there) was an excellent teacher, she loved being there, she loved learning, he was supportive, engaging and it was a terrific experience. We also had terrible experiences, teachers controlling every moment of the day, punishing for speaking, limiting recess.

In the years that I took my children in and out of school I heard a wide opinion from teachers about our choice to homeschool. A few told me I was making the biggest mistake of our life, while the majority said if they had known it was an option years ago, they would have done it with their own children.

In these days of chaos, whether a child was in school or not, I continued to educate myself about education. The history of our current educational system was eyeopening yet obvious once I had learned it. The late 1800's brought our current system of schools as a way to watch over children so that parents could work during the Industrial Revolution. The schools mimicked a factory setting, training young people for the assembly line work. Clocking in and out, listening to bosses/ teachers, answering to bells. What we see in education today, is only a century or so old. It is so interesting to me how we can so quickly believe as a society that the way we do things is the 'right' way, simply because it is how it is done.

And so, I held my book club group, with the sun shining through the large bay window we sat on mismatched wooden chairs with children of all ages playing all around us. We discussed Charlotte Mason. The book I had read and enjoyed was a companion to a series of classic books written by a woman in the late 1800's. She believed that education was a part of life, and they should not be considered separately.

The key piece I took away from her philosophy, was that learning is a science of relations. In my own words this means that when you are presented with new information, you take in what you can based on what knowledge you already have. She considered much of what we use to educate children twaddle - empty, useless information. Pam can sit. These books are simple and unnecessary. She preferred the idea of reading heavy classics to children and letting them glean what they could.

Charlotte Mason also loved the outdoors. I loved her opinion that nature needed to be a part of every day.

Overall, she was my first introduction to child-led education.

Our book club discussing her was full of parents similar to me, in that they all struggled with the system, loved knowledge and wanted what was best for our children. All of these parents had children in and out of school. We were trying to find our solutions while in the middle of it all.

This is when I was introduced to two more books/ philosophies that inspired me: the first was *A Well-Trained Mind*.

At this point I had already learned to take what I loved about something and make it my own. I do not encourage you to pick one of these books and use it as your roadmap, although many do. I encourage you to read them all, find what you love and let that create your own philosophy.

A Well-Trained Mind by Susan Wise Bauer is a book that lays out what Classical Education looks like. It is a great introduction to what Classical Education is. In layman's terms it means using the classics, i.e. Shakespeare and Plato, to teach children to think and learn for themselves (you can see how this sparked my interest.) It has now become a full series with workbooks and tools for learning.

I loved the suggestion that to teach this you needed to learn it yourself first. I poured my energy into reading all of the classical literature they recommended, enjoying Beowulf to Jane Eyre.

My problem with the Well-Trained Mind series books, and Classical Education systems in general, was that they pushed the idea of penmanship and rigorous grammar with young children. I did not like making my children do that work. I wanted them to enjoy learning, not hate it like I had for so long.

Then two of the women at the book club introduced me to *A Thomas Jefferson Education* by Oliver DeMille. This book was a huge step forward for me, cementing my strong opinions about education and what was best for me as an educator and my children.

TJ Ed

Play builds the kind of free-and-easy, try-it-out, do-it-yourself character that our future needs.

-JAMES L HYMES, JR.

A Thomas Jefferson Education, or TJEd for short, is a philosophy based on a look back at how our founding fathers in America were educated before the current public school system was implemented. I have a long laundry list of issues with our founding fathers, but that is for another time. These books do seem to hold them in very high esteem. As I have said, take the yummy and true pieces for yourself, and leave the rest.

TJEd is about raising leaders. It is about raising individuals who are strong and independent. Man, I loved that. It relies on mentors and highlights freedom at every turn (many Libertarians friends came into my life here.)

The basic overview of TJEd is that there are phases of learning. We start in Core, where a young kid between the ages of approximately 3-7 is learning the difference between right and wrong, good and evil. It is a time to teach values and focus on the child's understanding of truth.

One of my favorite little nuggets from this section was when they explained that if a six-year-old is practicing their penmanship and you correct them, even kindly, "This A is wrong." They will internalize it, hearing 'you are wrong,' even, 'you are bad.' After my interactions with my own children, I saw this as a reality. And I loved the idea of reading fairy tales and playing make-believe, working with them on these core values. I wanted my children to be strong of character.

So, not much 'table time' learning for the Core Phase. The next phase was the Love of Learning Phase, ages approximately 8-12. This is just what it sounds like; have fun learning lots of exciting new stuff. Don't push it, just explore, until it isn't fun anymore.

This was so fun for me. This felt really like what I do. With ADHD I am constantly excited about new things. Our 'table time' made a comeback. When I was first learning about TJEd, both K— and T— were in this age group. We explored all sorts of fun things. I began doing unit studies, bringing all of the books I could find from the library home for us to look through together.

You might think that I had found just what I needed, but unfortunately, there are two more levels in TJEd. The Scholar Phase comes next, and this looked so much like Classical Education dressed up in a different color dress that I balked at it a bit. Now that your child is 12, they will be ready for 25-50 hours of uninterrupted study time. They make a contract with the student and suddenly because they are given responsibilities, they are a 'young adult' rather than just a 'teenager.'

Finally, TJ Ed has the Depth Phase starting at around age 16. This is when the student finds what they are passionate about and pour themselves into it. This is often done in a college setting they say. One story I really did like from this still means a lot to me, and I have told this one a bunch over the years.

If you put a little kid in front of a piano and start them on lessons. "Practice 20 minutes a day." Give them the beginner book. Take them to a teacher and have them rigorously stick to the routine, you will have by the age of 10 a young person who can read basic music and play songs. As an adult (here I am speaking from experience) they might be able to sit at any piano and play two separate songs as if they were a great pianist but ask them to play anything else and it has not stuck.

However, let's say a young man at sixteen gets excited about learning piano. They have never had a lesson before, but take that book and research, and play for hours a day. Within a few months they will have surpassed the young kid who religiously attended his lessons for years and whined at each daily practice. Their passion will push them to learn it quickly and much more completely. Interest in a topic is key to true learning and retention.

And so, life ticked by for us, and we moved again, and the kids just kept on getting older, and J— kept on working three jobs, and I kept on 24/7 with kid-os.

K— hit the Scholar Phase, and we tried some of these Scholar contracts. They didn't work. She was already doing fine learning what she wanted to learn, and I was not good at the whole follow through part. While I do believe that Scholar Phase and Depth Phase happens, I don't believe that we need to make it happen, we don't need to create it or force it or put an age on it.

I was realizing that what my kids really needed was true freedom and trust - and that was what Unschooling was.

I Was Finally an All-In Unschooler

When you get down to it, unschooling is really
just a fancy term for 'life' or 'growing up
uninstitutionalized.'

- GRACE LLEWELLYN

It was around 2007 that I became a full-blown unschooler, confident in my decision. At the time my youngest, A— was 4, P— was 7, T— was 9, and K— was 13. I was 33 and finally felt in control of my life.

There had been so many years and decisions made in the moment, so many reactionary decisions. I was finally educated and comfortable with my own opinion. I stood my ground firmly. J— was on board, he always was, trusting in my decisions, or calling me out when needed. But when it came to unschooling, by this time, we were both all in.

We had found other families who were also unschooled, their children free to hang out with ours whenever they wanted. We found groups of people who accepted our decision even if they didn't unschool their own children.

My parents still questioned the choice. When the only question you ask children is "what are you learning in school right now?" You suddenly are at a loss with unschooled children. They switched it to "what are you reading now?" Still a tricky question when there were often times, the kids weren't reading anything. And although I had for years worried over what my family thought of my choices, I didn't anymore.

New homeschoolers often will tell me how they have to deal with strangers giving them a hard time about the choice to homeschool. It was at a cool spring play group that it hit me. I used to get accosted like that too. What had changed? My confidence.

When I was asked by strangers now about what we were doing, I didn't leave room for them to bring their concerns (unwarranted, and to be honest none of their business) to light. My confidence shut their advice down before they even got that far.

Our days, nights, weekends, summers all blended together. We lived and we learned, and most of all we played and had fun. The only rules in our home were:

1. Be nice to each other.

2. If playing a make-believe game everyone got to be whatever they wanted, and everyone had to figure it out. Yes, the pre-schooler can be a teenager. Yes, your brother can be a Digimon. Figure it out.

3. No Kardashians.

If you read a book on unschooling or ask an unschooled child or parent about what it means, you will get a million different definitions. There is extreme unschooling, there is radical unschooling, there is part time unschooling.

Here is mine.

Unschooling means leaving the system behind. Focusing on the child in the moment and what they need and want, with love and fun. Engaging with them where they are and showing through examples how to live and learn. Education suddenly becomes a continuation of the way all parents encourage their babies to take their first steps. When the kids ask a question, being happy to share an answer, or willing to say, "I don't know, let's see if we can find out."

Homeschooling Expert?

Do not train children in learning by force and harshness... but direct them to it by what amuses their minds, so that you may be better able to discover with accuracy the peculiar bent of the genius of each.

— PLATO

We were still a part of our secular homeschool group HOUSE, but over the years I had stepped into a leadership position. Probably a mix of both my social nature, and my time being freer since I wasn't doing school at home like many other families in the group.

Our local chapter of HOUSE was founded in the 70's and was part of a state-wide group of homeschool cooperatives. The state group has a website with tons of great information about the laws in the state of Illinois.

Homeschooling is regulated under state laws, so it is very dependent on where you live on how much freedom you have. There are some states that expect you to bring your children in and get them tested each year, there are others that expect the parents to be certified teachers. Illinois is one of the more relaxed.

The law expects that children be educated in the categories that the public schools teach and that they learn what children at their level are learning.

Spelling Power had taught me a lot, so had our experience with different schools. What a child learns in one second grade class is not exactly the same as what they learn in another. As long as my children were on a similar path, they would be fine. And I believed wholeheartedly that they would be fine in the end. I believed in unschooling.

Parents found the state site when they were falling out of school, and contacted the local HOUSE person, and that was me. I met with mothers and fathers who were like I had been five and ten years before. Worried, scared, unhappy- most of them knowing something was wrong, but not knowing what they could do about it. I talked people down from the fright and encouraged them to educate themselves. I met them at parks and libraries. Their children played with mine, and we all opened our eyes a bit more to the reality that schools are a mess.

One afternoon I had a phone interview with a woman from a local mom website (man, had times changed.) She was asking questions about homeschooling, and after ten years I had a lot of answers. They came easily to me now. I knew the court cases that solidified our state laws, I knew the types of homeschoolers, I knew the options for community support for families. I answered her questions standing in my kitchen with the kids running in and out playing, a normal day for us.

When the article was published, I was a bit floored. "Interview with Local Homeschooling Expert, Maya Gouliard."

Expert?

I felt insecure for a day or two and finally realized that I had to own it. I had become an expert in homeschooling.

I knew all of the curriculum choices, I knew all of the education styles from Montessori to Classical, from Traditional to Eclectic. And I chose to leave them all behind and unschool.

When new parents asked me about curricula and options, I always told them they needed to know what their goals were for their children.

"If you want your child to get into Harvard, your days are going to look much different than ours." I would say with a laugh.

If they were interested in what my goals were the answer was always the same. "I want my children to know who they are and know how to learn."

I did my best to tell them what they were ready to hear. "Each parent gets to decide for themselves what is best." Inside I was always screaming "just unschool! Let your kids become who they are, not who you want them to be." But I kept it quiet, rarely pushing my opinion on others.

I still got pushback from people saying I was a bad influence. Many considered unschoolers lazy, choosing it because they don't have to put in the work. But that is not the case. I put in a decade of work, learning, educating myself, reflecting on what I wanted for society and for my children and for myself. And I continued to put work in day in and day out with the kids, it just wasn't in a formal system. We were active everyday. I spent time with my kids from the moment we awoke until we went to sleep, and often in the middle of the night too.

Libraries & Parks

Children are adept at learning on their own, in their own way, if we allow them the space to do so. Be a student of your child, observing what strikes interest and curiosity in them. Trust and respect their natural ability to learn.

- DURENDA WILSON

There were a lot of people who questioned what we did with all of our time, but the days were full. We met other homeschoolers, did group classes that we thought were fun. But there were three places we spent most of our time: libraries, parks and game stores.

We spent so much time at parks. We were lucky to live in a place with two separate park districts, each with a multitude of parks. I made it a mission of mine to visit each one. We all had our favorites, and there was a list of part attributes we all agreed were important:

1. No big crowds
2. Not near a school
3. Bathrooms available
4. Nice picnic tables near the play area

Once a week our homeschool group met at a park. It was one of my family's jobs to coordinate this. It made sense for us to be in charge of it, because we were the most likely to be at each one, and also, because of my children's span in ages there was usually someone at the park around the age of another family's children. Other members were more likely to come if they knew a kid was there for their kid(s) to play with.

Being at every park day was also a reason I ended up in a leadership role. Park days were often the first group event new families would attend, so I was the one answering their questions.

Originally, we had called the meet ups at the park 'play dates.' But as my children got older, they were not excited about the name. So, I changed it to Park Days. But we didn't always meet at the park. In the cold months, or the super hot days, we would head to the library.

Libraries are the best resource out there for anyone who wants to learn. We found out quickly that our local library had a 200-item limit on what you could check out. I had a milk crate bin that we would carry in and the kids would excitedly fill it with books on anything they wanted . I would check out books I was inspired to share with them. We probably only read about 30% of what we brought home, but that was quite a bit. They loved asking the librarian for help finding books on Chinchillas, Pokémon, or whatever the most recent thrill was.

Libraries are also a great resource for space. Whether we were meeting a few friends to sit around on a cold winter afternoon, or if we had a large event/class with all of the families in HOUSE, the library had space for us. We were welcomed and encouraged by most librarians. There were a few who were always telling the kids to be quiet, but most libraries now have the children's department set up in a place where the quiet is not as important, and the passion is encouraged.

And talking about passion, we cannot forget about Game Stores. Local gaming shops are some of the best third spaces. Third spaces are defined as where you go when you aren't at work or home. Often, they are your community, think Churches or bars. A local game store is a great community space for families.

Our family was introduced to Magic: The Gathering in 2007. It was around the time I was embracing the idea to just have fun with the kids. We all played the game together and spent tons of hours at the game store. Board games, card games, puzzles, or just hanging out - games stores have it all. And they have snacks! In exchange for supporting them by buying an educational game, you get space at large tables to sit and play a game with friends.

Although there are a ton of third spaces in the community that welcome families, the place we spent the most time was home. Our home during these years was pretty much constant chaos. A— playing Minecraft on the computer in the kitchen, Hannah Montana on the TV in the living room with no one in there, music blasting from K— 's room, different music blasting from P— 's room, and T— playing Mario Kart in his room.

I think the point I want to make clear here is that we were generally always with each other. I spent a lot of quality time with them. We chatted about what was on TV, we talked about how cute the squirrels were running after each other at the park, we read books together on the big chairs at the library, we played Pokémon together. And although in the moment, it was chaos, when I look back now, it was heaven. Trust me, I know how cheesy that sounds, but it is 100% true.

So, wait, you ask. Was everything so perfect? How can we make it perfect?

No, absolutely not, things were not perfect, and no one can make it that way. We had toddler temper tantrums, sibling rivalry, teenage angst, all of the classics. Those are signs of growth in my opinion. They are all important pieces of the exploration of individuality. In the moment they are painful, and from the inside it feels like you are failing, but from the finish line, they are important moments where a lot of growth is happening. Not sure that helps, but maybe you can keep it in mind during the next time there is chaos at your dinner table.

Reading

Education is not the filling of a pail, but the lighting of a fire.

- WILLIAM BUTLER YEATS

Reading is such an important piece of education. It is the lens through which we learn so much. Nowadays, there are a lot of ways to learn through video, and I am so glad for that. I have learned so many topics on YouTube. However, books are a window into so much, from imagination to information.

I already shared about my childhood experience of my friends surpassing me and reading classics such as *The Princess Bride* and *The Secret Garden*, while I was still stuck reading Choose Your Own Adventure stories. That experience alone taught me that there was no rush. Many of the books I was reading on education spoke at length about how there was no correlation to early readers and long-term reading skills. In fact, many discussed children learning to read at nine or ten, were proven life-long learners.

I can't speak from anything but experience here, since I haven't done any in-depth research projects on this. For myself, as I was reading these books on education, I was also eating up the classics. In my thirties I read almost every book I found on the top 100 books of all time list. This became a lot more than 100 books, because every list I found had different books on it.

But let's talk about our kids. K— had struggled in first grade worried and stressed because she couldn't read at the level the other kids could. When we began homeschooling, the one-on-one time instantly buffeted her courage. She was actually reading very well, just felt what we might call stage fright about doing it in front of others.

K— was one of the lucky kids who was exactly the age/ reading level for the Harry Potter books. As she grew, the HP books were released, increasing in difficultly level, and it encouraged her love of reading.

The hoopla surrounding HP also encouraged it. I mean, there were parties at the library for each release, friends were reading it too, so it was social. The Harry Potter sensation really was something that I doubt will ever be experienced again. I want to quickly note that both of us were heartbroken as we learned of the author's extreme stance on the wrong side of many issues we care about, it really is awful.

T— learned to read from video games, specifically Paper Mario. The Paper Mario games are super fun, and I recommend them to anyone who loves a good story and humor. They are two dimensional characters in a three-dimensional world, and there are a lot of comic book style text on the screen. T— started playing video games at two and loved running little Mario around climbing trees and jumping off. By the time he was 5 he could play and beat most games, but he needed help with the reading. And occasionally a few of the big bosses were too hard, so mom came to help.

I would read the words on the screen, or take the controller and whap, bam, boom - beat whoever he couldn't. It was definitely good for our relationship, lol. He respected me. But he also got tired of waiting for me to be available to come when he needed to know what the characters were saying. I also had his sisters to do things with.

He would spell the words out to me from another room, and I would sound it out with him, until eventually, he was just reading it himself. He never really got into reading books, but he did occasionally. Diary of a Wimpy Kid was one of his favorites.

P— had gone to kindergarten and already we had learned that she was taking her time with reading. She wasn't too interested in learning her letters. I found that she was like me, and would often confuse different letters, or draw them backwards. I have never been diagnosed, and neither has she, but I'm pretty sure we both have dyslexia.

Oh no, dyslexia! Didn't that mean we had to go to a reading expert? No. All we needed was patience and understanding.

Encouraging someone with dyslexia to read is simply about taking their time. It isn't about finishing the book quickly. It is about reading at the pace your brain can take it in. I often will read a sentence and think, "well, that makes absolutely no sense." The ironic thing is that I can read it two or three times and read the same thing again and again. My brain will see a word wrong each time. The slower I read the more likely I am to read correctly. As an experienced adult who understands what is happening, I now know that when that happens, I have to look at each word separately. I usually find a word that was completely different than what I had initially thought. A 'how' becomes a 'who' and everything is right again in the world.

With P— my experience helped me guide her to slow her pace and enjoy the experience. She loved picture books, and we would read together taking turns, she might read a page and then be done and go play or she might sit and listen to me.

I read to all of the kids aloud a lot. We read big books, the classics as a group, I read picture books at bedtime.

Anytime they wanted a story read to them, my answer was yes. Did I limit how many at bedtime? Rarely, we didn't have anywhere to be first thing in the mornings. Often bedtime books were some of our best times, cuddled up and enjoying a good story for hours.

Reading aloud is one of the best teachers. Slowly sounding out words when they are at the learning stage. The more interest they show in the actual words on the page, the more I would point and sound it out. Letting them join me.

One of my favorite reading stories is about our youngest. A— was just along for the ride as a little one. She got all of the blessings of unschooling, because by the time she was a toddler, I was already educated and ready to do this. She had really wanted to go to school though, so at 5 she started kindergarten, but she quickly found it was not what she wanted. She wanted her brother to be there too. The teacher was fine with us having T— join for a few days to see if it helped her transition, but we all quickly realized that school was just not what she had expected and she was home again within a few weeks. So aside from that short experience, A— was 100% unschooled.

She never felt the push to read by a certain time. She never experienced the test that made her struggle. She just enjoyed reading with all of the family. Her siblings would read to her at the library, and I read to her every night, and often during the day. She pulled armfuls of books off of the library shelf and we enjoyed reading about distant places, adorable animals, fairies and more.

One day when she was around 7, we were in the car. She was sitting in her little booster chair in the back seat and reading words on the billboards. Impressed, I told her, "You are doing a great job! You are such a great reader."

"But I can't read yet."

"A—, you just read that word back there. And you always read the stop signs, and what does that say there?" I asked

"Well, I know that word." She said, "but I don't know that one there yet."

She had thought that she couldn't say she was a reader until she knew ALL the words. T— was kind enough to explain to her that you don't have to know every word to know how to read, no one can know every word.

What a weighty responsibility to know every single word.

So, to get back on track, reading is super important. It is the key to much learning. But so often we treat it like a chore. We definitely treat teaching as a chore. Practice this, practice that. I find it was simple to teach when we just enjoyed books together, slowly transitioning to them enjoying the stories on their own sometimes.

We humans are all innately curious, and curiosity is the best encouragement for learning.

Screen Time

It is a happy talent to know how to play.

- RALPH WALDO EMERSON

I want to devote a whole chapter to screen time, because I was a bit unique in my opinions compared to the parents around us. So many people worry over screen time. Even unschoolers I have interacted with, who give their children freedom in all other aspects of their lives, controlled the screen.

We did not.

There were times when we as a family decided to turn the TV's off and focus on something, but I never said, "Only one hour of screen time a day."

When cell phones began to be an item the kids carried around, I did start by taking it away at bedtime (again, poor K— the Guinea pig.) until I realized I was just causing myself and them pain.

Let me tell you a story about some adults - I have heard this same story twice from two different people. The first was one of my very best friends, and the second was about the husband of a friend. Both of these adults had grown up in homes without televisions. Now, as adults they could not be in public spaces with TV's without being sucked in. Out to dinner, when a television was on, they would be watching it, not interacting with their spouse or friends.

We would invite families over and the children who had limited screen time at home would be sucked into the TV's, choosing to stare at the screen rather than interact and play. I even remember parents asking me to turn off the TVs in our home. I usually did, but life isn't going to do that for them in every setting.

On the flip side. My children were allowed to watch almost anything they wanted; they were not limited on the time spent with a television on. They were not limited on video games, or computer time. And yet, when a friend came over, they were quick to leave the screens behind; when a neighborhood kid knocked on the door, they were quick to drop what they were doing and play tag; when given the choice to do something else, it was simple to walk away from the screen. There was no fear that it was their only chance to enjoy what the screen had.

The same thing can be said about food and soda. My son used to play video games at his computer and would have a stack of chip bags and soda cans. Then, at about the age of 14, he told me he was done. He quit drinking soda. To this day, he limits the amount of soda he takes in.

My husband was a cook, and food was a family affair in our home. I think family dinner is one of the best things ever invented, and if you can't homeschool, at least eat dinner together. At the time, there were serious stresses about dinners in our home. Each child eating different items. My daughters all went through serious vegetarian/vegan eras. Was it a bit of a nightmare and added to the chaos? Of course. But they were learning about nutrition, they were caring about food, they were involved in the cooking and choices.

Limiting, like forcing, from my experience, often has the opposite effect long term. I was raising little individuals and celebrating people understanding what is best for themselves. I encourage you to trust your little ones to make these choices (whether good or mistakes) young, so they can learn from them with you there.

Socialization - Who is it Important to Spend Time With?

School prepares for the alienating institutionalization of life by teaching the need to be taught.

— IVAN ILLICH

There are some questions you hear over and over again as a homeschooler. I have answered them so many times that when people ask me now, I generally don't even want to continue the conversation. I will give them a short and sweet basic answer. I want to delve in a bit more here to the most asked question of all.

What about socialization? How will your children learn to get along with others? It's not always phrased this way, sometimes they will simply ask about being around other kids their age, or learning how to stand in line of all things.

One time I was interviewed on camera for a local news program about homeschooling. Talk about nerve racking. I had been answering questions to parents for years, talking comfortably with strangers for my jobs as a server or cashier, or in smaller intimate settings with people who were genuinely interested. This TV studio was another matter.

Suddenly, as someone who has rolled out of bed my whole life and rarely worn make up, I was worried about what I looked like. I was stressed about what they were going to ask. I was worried that the other parents in the group interview would judge me. I was dealing with a super fun run of anxiety.

The interview only lasted about ten minutes, and with three of us there, I was only asked a few questions. I did fine most of the time, however, one of the questions was about finding other homeschoolers in the area. My answer was something along the lines of, "there are more homeschoolers around than people realize, I could probably throw a stick and hit a homeschooler." In my mind it sounded awkward, but J— when hearing it later thought it sounded like I wanted to hit homeschoolers with sticks. Let's just say, I will not be choosing to do any more news interviews.

My point with the stick had been that after I became more familiar with homeschooling and the community, I found homeschoolers everywhere. In all three of the homes we lived in, we found a homeschooled family within 2 blocks of us. There really are a lot of homeschoolers in our country. The official numbers are impossible to come by, because a lot choose not to fill out any paperwork, and in our state, at least, it isn't mandatory.

So, we could find a family nearby that gives you at least one kid to play with, but what about groups? Well, I have spoken before about HOUSE. Although you must remember HOUSE is only one of the community groups supporting families, there are tons of them. Some are just a few families working as a team. Some of them are church based and build off of the community already there. Some are classroom based, meeting much like the modern schools we are all familiar with, but only one or two days a week, with parents teaching classes.

At HOUSE events, our children were placed into groups spanning all ages. One of my favorite parts about park day was when a group of about 15 kids would traipse off into the small, wooded area near where the parents sat. The group would range in age from pre-k to high school, and they all had fun together. We always had at least one older kid who would decide to hang out with the parents each day, joining in the conversation.

This all demonstrates the magic to me - and highlights one of the flaws of our modern schools - inter-generational communication. In public schools you spend time with about twenty kids within a year of your age. You interact with fewer than ten adults in that year, and all of them are in a strong authority position, not to mention over-worked, on the clock, and answering to a curricula and bell system. It is very difficult to have those magical moments of getting close to someone, when all of that is hanging over your head.

My children loved talking to all ages. They brought the little ones along and played with them, learning to teach. They talked about nutrition, games, and life with their favorite parents. It has encouraged them to find mentors in life now as adults also.

There was a parent in our group who had two teenage boys around my son's age. They had just recently fallen out of school and were still learning how to break from the system they were used to. Once we were all five in the car together. The mother was talking about trying to set up something that would be just for teenagers. As she was trying to make her point, she said, "T— wouldn't you like to get away from all of the little kids sometimes?" T— just shook his head and said, "I don't mind them being around." Coming from a teenager, this was high praise. I was so proud of him at that moment.

And back to learning to stand in line and follow society's standards. They learn that when out in public. They learn from the example of others in society. You don't have to line up quietly in the hallways ten times a day to learn how to wait your turn at the grocery store.

But What About Math?

There is no difference between living and learning... it is impossible and misleading and harmful to think of them being separate.

—JOHN HOLT

I would say the most divisive topic out of everything brought up in my choice was math. Let's address this head on, starting with teaching young people math concepts.

When we first began I had the workbooks and math manipulatives, work sheets, and practice exams. I sat and did my best to patiently explain ones, tens and hundreds and carry the one to a six-year-old. The thing that really frustrated me was how upset they were with themselves that it didn't make sense to them. They wanted to know why. They wanted to grasp all of the minutia and reasoning behind this problem, but it was beyond them. And no matter the time we spent with the tiny one's places blocks and the ten's rod and the hundreds square and the thousands 3-d cube, it wasn't clicking.

With our third child, I was already slowing down any pressure. I remember first tackling the concept when she was closer to eight. It clicked instantly. There were no frustrating sighs, there were no busy-work worksheets to practice a concept that wasn't sinking in. She just understood and was quickly able to solve the problems.

This was when one of our biggest issues came up though. Friends of my children's who were still entrenched in the traditional public-school model were telling them how terrible it was that they didn't know their times tables at a certain point or that they didn't work on math for an hour a day. These people put the seed of doubt into my young children's happy days, and I was so upset.

My opinion (and I realize that this is an opinion, like much of this book) is that much of the math work our children do in the traditional school setting is busy-work set to fill the days with 'active learning.' What we found from our personal experiences, and seeing other kids in the classrooms, was that children who weren't ready were falling further behind because they were stuck on a simple small math fact and the rest of the class was pushing on ahead, while the students not understanding just kept on not understanding. I think this is a common issue with the standardized testing and strict calendar approach to education.

Let's talk a bit about math in everyday life. The fact is math is everywhere, and our children are immersed in it, simply by living. You want to buy a candy bar at the gas station? Here's $5, bring me the change. You want to bake cookies, here's a measuring cup. It's a 1/4 cup and you need 3/4 cups of sugar. We aren't going to the library until 10:00. What time is it now? They learned to answer these math questions through living life. Sometimes they would ask me to help them understand and we would use worksheets, they are very useful tools when a child is actively excited about learning, and ready for the content.

What about algebra, and calculus? Higher math is important too. Aren't you holding your child back? To this I am going to bring up some of my lowest points in homeschooling. I went through this with all of my four children. They were teenagers and they were mad. They were mad at the world and me, and almost every time they were mad, they brought up math. They were worried about going out into a world where they wouldn't fit in and everyone else would know things that they didn't. I understood their worries, but I still felt, as I do today, that it was the right choice.

My oldest really wanted to go to college. I fully supported her. College courses are a fantastic resource for someone who knows why they want to be there and understands the cost and if it is worth it to them. She was very worried about math. Guess what happened? Let's think back to my story of the person learning piano because they were invested - the same thing happened. She took the placement test and was placed in Math 98. She took a few college courses and within two semesters had learned what she needed to. And were the classes empty? Were they only full of unschoolers? No, they had adults who had either forgotten, or students who had never understood it in the public-school setting.

My other three have not gone on to college, and with the cost of it nowadays, I support them in their choices. They have all seen the state of the real world now. They no longer worry that they don't know enough math to survive as adults. For example, working in jobs that deal with cash, they have seen other public schooled employees struggle with counting a drawer, while my kids picked it up. In fact, many of the young adults I speak with now laugh at how ridiculous it is that they learned so much math in school, but not how to do their taxes.

Math is just one example of how if you follow your passions, you can really learn whatever you want, when you are ready.

Beyond 'School'

What we learn with pleasure we never forget

– ALFRED MERCIER

I really don't like the name unschool. It doesn't do how unschoolers educate justice. There is such a focus on <u>school</u>. Home *school*. *School* at home. De *school*. Public *school*. Private *School*. Un*school*. It just dehumanizes the experience. It also skews any discussion based on what we all, in this day and age, see as school and education in general.

Education is not the same as school, just as religion is not the same as a church. But when we use those words, our mind envisions what we already know of the concepts.

My journey in educating myself about education was intense, exciting and eyeopening. I knew I had doubts about how our traditional public schools were doing things, because I had struggled so much where my sisters had thrived. I saw from a young age the cracks in the system.

That allowed my mind to be open to these new concepts. It encouraged me to look for something different. There are times now when people ask me about my experience homeschooling. I can see within thirty seconds or so, if they they are open to listening to what we actually did, or if they just won't get it. It took my dad and stepmom about ten years to understand what I was doing. My mom and stepdad still don't really understand my decision, or what it meant. And that's okay, I didn't do it for them.

I had two goals raising my children. That they would know who they were, and that they would know how to learn. I can happily say that I accomplished those goals. I have four adults in my life now, that are the most unique and fascinating people.

The cover of this book is an art piece I made after I had embraced this new educational philosophy. The white paper cranes lined up in the picture frame represented the status quo to me, students boxed in and expected to look the same, face the same direction, work to the same goals - and the few who escape getting to fly free and become the best version of themselves, becoming a colorful array of unique human beings. These represented my own children, raised with a different outlook, a view beyond the boxes traditional schools place children in.

But I accomplished something that wasn't on my list too. It wasn't until they had all moved out, that I realized

Our Journey into Unschooling

I have no regrets about time - in the years, and minutes I spent with them. I don't look back and wish I had done more. I don't look back and think, if only I had a better relationship with them. There is nothing quite so validating in my past decisions than the regular texts and phone calls, and the genuine trust and love I still get from them today.

I didn't write this book to tell you what to do. I wrote it because we did something rare, and it is good for people to hear these types of stories. I try my best to be supportive of individuality, and the right for each person, parent, family to do what they think is best. But I think it would be false of me not to be honest here. I truly believe that child-led, (adult-led, individual-led) education is the best. Unschooling, done with love and genuine support is the best.

So, my advice? Read about education. Talk to mentors. Learn, and be sure to have fun along the way.

It is only fair to let the students have their say. Where are they now? What are their thoughts looking back?

Their answers follow. Maybe someday one of them will write their own book about it.

Looking Back: K—

Life is a game, play it.

— MOTHER TERESA

What is your current age, and can you sum up briefly what life looks like for you nowadays?

I am 30 years old and just moved to Charlotte NC from my hometown. I'm settling into my new home and city by working as a bartender and trying to keep busy by traveling, trying out different yoga studios, and meeting up with new friends. I'm also trying to make time for solitude so I can make art and rest.

What is your favorite memory from the days we unschooled?

My favorite memories were likely at playgroup. I enjoyed spending time with the wide range of people who came. The babies and toddlers were the best.

What hurdles have you run into as an adult because you were unschooled?

Catching up in math once I got to college was really difficult.

What is your least favorite part of having been unschooled?

Not knowing pop culture references.

Maya Gouliard

Are you glad you unschooled as a child?

Yes.

Would you unschool your own children?

Not fully but partially, yes.

Looking Back: T—

You can discover more about a person in an hour of play than in a year of conversation.

— PLATO

What is your current age and can you sum up briefly what life looks like for you nowadays?

26, Pretty standard life. Spend lots of time working and relaxing at home with my girlfriend.

What is your favorite memory from the days we unschooled?

Not very specific but just days spent in the park or game store were the best. Also playing games with my friends in the library.

What hurdles have you run into as an adult because you were unschooled?

A lot of social awkwardness. It's gotten much better over the past few years though as I've learned and experienced more.

What is your least favorite part of having been unschooled?

Social stigma and awkwardness around social situations.

Are you glad you unschooled as a child?

I had a long phase where I wasn't happy with it. These days I've come to accept it and appreciate it for what it was. Now I'm happy with it overall.

Would you unschool your own children?

I would not.

Looking Back: P—

Life must be lived as play.

- PLATO

What is your current age and can you sum up briefly what life looks like for you nowadays?

I'm 24 and I am a single mother living in Hawaii with lots of friends/community help.

What is your favorite memory from the days we unschooled?

"Park day" / playgroup

What hurdles have you run into as an adult because you were unschooled?

None

What is your least favorite part of having been unschooled?

My mom let me decide if I wanted to go to school or not and I decided I did want to go but sometimes I wish she wouldn't have let me go because most of my traumas came from being in school. But overall, I am grateful for the person that I am today so I am overall grateful for all my experiences that made me who I am.

Are you glad you unschooled as a child?

Yeah

Would you unschool your own children?

Yeah

Any additional thoughts you'd like to share?

The biggest reason for me wanting to go to school was for socializing. If there was a bigger unschool/homeschool community or more structured ways I could've been around other kids/people I probably wouldn't have cared to go to public school. I'm ultimately really grateful for my perspective of being able to be in public school with the knowing that I "had" to be there

Looking Back: A—

Thank goodness I was never sent to school; it would have rubbed off some of the originality.

- BEATRIX POTTER

What is your current age and can you sum up briefly what life looks like for you nowadays?

I am 21 married and working as a server

What is your favorite memory from the days we unschooled?

Sledding in winter and the library

What hurdles have you run into as an adult because you were unschooled?

Anxiety

What is your least favorite part of having been unschooled?

(Same answer as above)

Are you glad you unschooled as a child?

Sometimes yes, sometimes no

Would you unschool your own children?

No

Books Referenced in this Memoir

Adams-Gordon, Beverly L., 2004. *Spelling Power*: Castlemoyle Books

Andreola, Karen, 1998. *A Charlotte Mason Companion: Personal Reflections on the Gentle Art of Learning*:Charlotte Mason Research & Supply co.

Bauer, Susan Wise, 2004. *The Well Trained Mind*: W.W. Norton & Company

DeMille, Oliver, 2009. *A Thomas Jefferson Education:* TJEdOnline.com

Llewelyn, Grace, 1997. *The Teenage Liberation Handbook: How to Quit School and Get a Life*: Turtleback

About the Author

Author Newsletter : www.mayagouliard.substack.com

Author Website : www.mayagouliard.com

Maya Gouliard is a renaissance woman, serial entrepreneur, and lifelong learner with an insatiable curiosity for new experiences. With a Master's degree in Recreation, Sport and Tourism and a focus on leisure studies, she brings a unique perspective to conversations about purposeful living and creative pursuits.

As an empty-nester after raising four children through unschooling (which she chronicled in her memoir), Maya has reinvented herself multiple times—owning a restaurant, running a Magic: The Gathering game store, publishing fantasy novels, and creating handmade quilts for craft markets. Her journey navigating ADHD has taught her to embrace her multi-passionate nature rather than fight it.

Now, with her grandson bringing new joy to her life and 28 years of marriage providing perspective, Maya writes, sews and hosts the podcast "I've Always Got Time to Talk," where she explores the intersection of creativity, entrepreneurship, education, and living life on your own terms—especially in midlife and beyond.

Also by Maya Gouliard

CHROMA Series

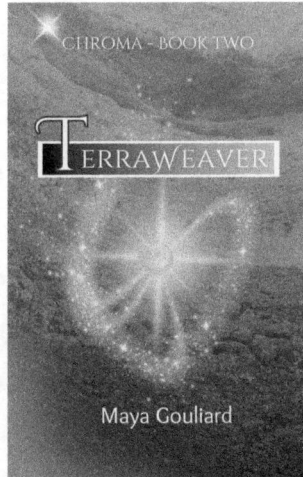

After raising four children on the limited resources of the Wastelands, Lara must venture out to Azural, the blue realm where she hopes to return the water magic to her village.

Her adventures will teach her all about the changes to her world since the weavers first found the stones. But it will also teach her about herself and all she is capable of.

And did I forget to mention the baby dragon?

www.ingramcontent.com/pod-product-compliance
Lightning Source LLC
LaVergne TN
LVHW021615080426
835510LV00019B/2578